piano

First published in 2011 by
The Dedalus Press
13 Moyclare Road
Baldoyle
Dublin 13
Ireland

www.dedaluspress.com

Editor: Pat Boran

Copyright © Eva Bourke, 2011

ISBN 978 1 906614 40 9

All rights reserved.
No part of this publication may be reproduced in any form or by
any means without the prior permission of the publisher.

Dedalus Press titles are represented in the UK by
Central Books, 99 Wallis Road, London E9 5LN
and in North America by Syracuse University Press, Inc.,
621 Skytop Road, Suite 110, Syracuse, New York 13244.

Illustrations and cover art by Miriam de Búrca,
design by Benjamin de Búrca and Barbara Wagner.

The Dedalus Press receives financial assistance from
The Arts Council / An Chomhairle Ealaíon

piano

Eva Bourke

DEDALUS PRESS
DUBLIN, IRELAND

ACKNOWLEDGEMENTS

Acknowledgements are due to the editors of the following publications where a number of these poems first appeared:

The Irish Times ('Evening near Letterfrack', 'Snow Story', 'The Morning After'); *The Stinging Fly* ('The Soul of the Piano'), *Best Irish Poems 2010*. ed. Matthew Sweeney ('Achill Killeen'); *Dublin Poetry Review* ('A View of Berlin'); *The SHOp* ('Jardin Botanico'); *'Poetry Ireland Review'* Issue 100. ed. Paul Muldoon ('Last Seen'); *Sirena 2010*, Johns Hopkins Univ. Press: ed. Jorge Sagastuma ('Gardens', 'The Poet in his eighties', 'Poem for Stella Rotenberg', 'Homage'); *Sirena 2008*. ed. Jorge Sagastuma ('The Walk-in Heart'); *literaturwekstatt berlin. lyrik.org* ('The Heart of Things', 'Snow Story', 'Notes from Henry Street'); *Cúirt 2010 photographic exhibition* ('Class Photograph'); *Light Years—a Tribute to Pearse Hutchinson* ('I Woke to Sviatoslav Richter') *and Broadsheet on the occasion of Leland Bardwell's birthday* ('The Drowned Book').

Contents

I: The Soul of the Piano

& / 11
I Woke to Sviatoslav Richter / 13
A View of Berlin / 14
The Soul of the Piano / 17
Boston Underground Haiku / 18
Cricket Revisited / 19
Palermo Nocturne / 21
In the mornings always start with the sea / 23
Swifts / 24
Dawn Chorus in Late April / 25

II: The Grass Garden

Gardens / 29
Achill Killeen / 32
Bonfire Weeds / 34
Stendhal Syndrome / 36
The Grass Garden / 38
In the Garden of Images / 40
The Garden at the Road's End / 42
The Morning After / 43
Jardin Botanico / 44
Chinese Garden / 46

III: Travelling with Ruby

The poet at eighty takes out the 17 colours / 51
Homage / 53
The poet at ninety writes a letter / 55
Evening near Letterfrack / 57
Four People on a Lake / 59
The Spider Revisited / 61
Feeding Time / 63
Travelling with Ruby / 66

IV: The Heart of Things

Notes from Henry Street / 71
Last Seen / 73
Orplid / 75
The Heart of Things / 76
As if mid-tilt / 80
Stations / 82
A History of Photography / 84
August Near Südstern / 89
Elementary Poem / 90

V: Journal from the Mirrored Cities

Journal from the Mirrored Cities / 95
The Drowned Book / 108
Lacrimae rerum / 110
Snow Story / 111
Memoir / 112
Kōan / 113
The Piano Player's Resumé / 115

NOTES / 117

> Sing of the violated world
> and the grey feather lost by the thrush
> and the soft light that roams and vanishes
> and returns.
> —Adam Zagajewski

> The five strings say we can trust something else.
> And they accompany us a small part of the way there.
> As when the lights go out in the stairwell and the hand follows—
> trustingly—the blind handrail that guides through the dark.
> —Tomas Tranströmer

*for Ono,
our children,
grandchildren
and 'third grandchildren'*

I

The Soul of the Piano

&

Even the simplest beginning requires an initial ceremony,
must be courteously prepared—three saints, seated in
    comfortable intimacy,
converse within the figured initial, the first letter on the
    manuscript page,
framed by the flamboyant interlacing of a rose bower, each flower,
each petal and leaf an alpha of commencement inked in red
and black, then followed by the application of gesso and after
    that gold leaf,
rubbed and burnished until the saints' halos illuminate
the dark scriptorium alcove. It's winter and through the diamonds
of the window panes a thin ray of the setting sun catches
on the gold, the visible breath of the apprentice scribe who has
    put on
his fingerless mittens and lit a candle to continue work
on the precise minuscules of the sentence he just began scripting—
every now and again using the ligature & that stands for *and,*
this small word, old as speech and mathematics, durable, a
    plank thrown
over a stream onto which a chanting procession will set foot
one by one, a bridge on a chasm that lovers stride across
unaware of the world's disarray and noise, or singing in the wheels
of a train speeding from station to station. When we turn off
the light and music to go to our room, arms around each other,
pausing for a moment at the landing window to take
a look at the night sky, a parchment page primed and roughened
with chalk and ash on which minuscules flash like Carolingian
    silver
set at random among the ink-black initials of the cosmos,
you tell me of the scribe in his nocturnal scriptorium who
    invented the ligature &,
splicing the two letters of the Latin word *et* from sheer exhaustion,

just as when we hold each other, and you, taller by a few inches,
tiredly lean into me and I embrace you, we form together
a sign, interlaced, infrangible, and you say how his quill repeatedly
slipped from his grasp although he did amuse himself by drawing
drolleries on the margins—cartwheeling dragons and monkeys—
and how he is asleep now with his face on the book amidst jars
of red and blue paint, knives, reeds and lead points,
the benign smell of ink: *et* he has written again
and again, *et* in long columns marching like spiders down
the page, the second letter more and more aslant from tiredness,
entwined with the first for support, making one sign out of two.

I Woke to Sviatoslav Richter

I woke to Sviatoslav Richter playing Bach:
the English Suite VI.
The early morning spilled over
the city's cornices and sills.

It was October, still mild,
the air filled with the smell of vegetal decay;
trees in the street were turning colour,
golden, russet, flaming-red,

passers-by chatted and laughed
below my window.
Bach was on the air, each note rose
out of the black body

of the radio, weightless
and unerring on its way:
in the hanging gardens above the city
evil was unheard of,

fear and hate stood and listened,
pain and despair halted
their progress
through hospital wards.

The left hand knew precisely
where the right was going,
justice was justice,
truth and love were one,

soul rested against soul
beneath the wild cataracts.

A View of Berlin

A Turner sunset. Descent of late-May night, wispy grey
fabrics are lowered over rooftops, dreary post-war
tower blocks. Darkness embraces the lindens,
their diadems splendid and intricate as Gothic spires,
flows otter-sleek through arches, leans
in doorways, open windows, encircles all. The past
never comes to an end here, a coal barge chugging
upstream drags a long memorandum in its wake,
Cyrillic lettering crinkles the slick surface.

Boats moored to the Spree banks rock on the backwash,
the small waves slap and buffet the hulls.
Seated on deck where a confluence of tributaries causes
the sluggish river to widen and slip through a series
of locks, all sparkle and obsidian lustre, we watch
tourist boats being lifted to the next level,
strings of light bulbs looped around prow and rail,
people in summer gear stride across bridges and the bright
trains stream past along tall, spindly elevations.

Dressed up in flimsy stuffs, diaphanous and dusky,
the new-fangled city drowses on the opposite bank,
a mirage, where Mosquitos, Halifaxes once swooped
across the black-out streets spilling their cargos.
Traffic sounds are muted, discreet as the song
the night hums to itself. On the squat complacent
turret of the Palace of Justice a corona of warning lights
signals stern sentences to all, and the bulky
star-tipped domes go off and on disputing

eternally. War hides nearby in a basement room
busy drafting a memoir, a work in progress,
bending low over the latest murderous chapters.
And now the night releases its spillage of black
oil and the gas lanterns lining the long
streets spread the dim glow of bad
memories. Again the rough drafts of yet
another beginning—but how could one on such nights,
you ask, imagine the perfect machinery of control

that severed the river once, barbed wire, mines
watch towers, guards, guns spelling death to anyone
brave or foolish enough to attempt swimming
across. It became a graveyard. So many tragedies,
so many lost. The lists state: drowned, shot—or both.
Between high-rises on the island near us where fire-storms
had blazed devouring house by house, enshrined
in the lindens' tabernacle, a nightingale suddenly
strikes up its midnight song, hidden, we think,

among the topmost branches or in a tangle
of willows on the far bank, singing at
the behest of a forgotten minor godhead passing
through en route somewhere: the god of reed pipes,
cat calls, piccolo flutes, the god of street-gang
whistles, radio Warsaw signature tunes,
the god of trills and grace notes, in the guise of a Venetian
youth, descant or altus: the dulcet staves
of a wordless *miserere* that echo in the lofts of the night clouds

an oboe d'amore at odds with the percussive bass notes
of the traffic, calling across distances as the world goes round
on tiptoe forgetting all about its business,
the handsome woman at the table near us who's been

relating a litany of loss to her friend raises
her head and falls silent to hear the bird's
ringing affirmations, a group of Russian tourists
in the prow quietly put down their drinks, all of us
listen as to a child calling outside the window,

insistent, melodious, to return to the unmutilated
garden, place of leaf shadow, of forbearance, secrets
and unrestrained singing among willows, scrub, weeds,
nettles, wild angelica, buttercups, tangled grasses;
even the no-nonsense waitress busy clearing
away the glasses stands still beneath a flickering
halo of night moths that circle the deck lamp, talking
to herself as though trying to solve a mystery,
a question not even the merciful night can answer.

The Soul of the Piano

THE SOUL OF THE PIANO smells of damp backyards, potato soup, harbour bars after rain, of school rooms, war and gun powder, perfume and palace gardens in spring. I caress the piano's soul, which is black and white in equal measure; sometime it is covered in ashes, sometimes gold leaf, I caress its varnished back, place a velvet cloth over it and listen to it breathe deeply, its strings tightened to tearing point. More than half a century ago, the soul of the piano came floating upstream on the Danube from the Black Sea - my father sailed it as it sang of the source of rivers and long dusty summer roads. My father was nine years old and wore a sailor suit and a boater with a blue ribbon. A Swabian cabinet-maker fished them out, built a lidded box for the soul of the piano, told it that its task was resonance and obedience and propped it upright against the wall of his tool shed. After my father had fled to live in the desert where he studied papyrus scrolls by starlight, it was abandoned and forgotten. Bats hung upside down asleep in its reverberating coffin-black case. Spiders, dragging their silken threads behind them, walked all over it and it fell into a long sleep wrapped in cobwebs, bat droppings and sawdust. Sometimes there was a faint echo of faraway bells in the shed. Sometimes a string snapped when rats marched on the broken keys. In a dream the soul of the piano danced in Warsaw streets and knelt on the Place de la Concorde amidst horse-dung and blood. It dreamed of storms, of thunder and hail showers, it dreamed of spring mornings. Once a young woman in pain from a broken heart said a name and the name stayed in the soul of the piano forever. Another time a man sick unto death dressed in coat tails with bloodied shirtfront played it more beautifully than anyone had ever played it. A magician from Africa cast a spell on it and it flew across continents like a comet releasing a trail of glittering notes. Sometimes the soul sheds its case and remembers how to use its keys to open all conceivable locks on earth.

Boston Underground Haiku

Downtown Crossing rush hour,
a young black woman busker
plays her saxophone—Bach *Invention No. 3*

Midnight at Back Bay station,
the slow movement of
the *Moonlight Sonata*

Park Street outbound train,
Love Walked In, on the keyboard,
stacks of blue CDs

35° in the shade, a boy
waiting for the Orange line hums
Sweet and Slow to sleeping twin babies

Dawn in Harvard Square station
on the escalators two drunks
sing *Mack the Knife* in harmony

Cricket Revisited

1

Cricket, hidden in a crack
of the park gate's brick wall,
all summer passing on my bike
I heard you call:
crrrk crrrk crrrk,
a creaking door, a prayer wheel.

Now all is still,
no oracular voice, no wisecrack.
The air suddenly feels cool.

Time soon
for the October moon,
fat and round as a melon
to launder gold on
the roof tiles of the town.

2

Cricket, did you know
how silent we were—how
the dog-soiled park, the sick
lindens, the dusty trick-
le in the fountain
and I on my way home

from a music-filled hall
listened to your tale
of green leaves and clear
water? How
thirsty we were?
No three-tiered choir,
no orchestra, drum, or oboe
could rival your untiring fervor.

3

Praise crickets and their solitary music.
Praise crevices in the brick
of park gates. Praise
dry sounds raised in intervals
of night on crumbling stone, praise
stone and night and persistent calls.

Praise the ardour of musical wings.
Praise frayed acoustic wings.
After the turmoil, the happenings,
the summer night spun on its hinge. I heard
the cricket at the gate and stood.
Praise the single note of love affirmed

in the summer night. Praise rough voices raised
to sing. Unfaltering song be praised.

Palermo Nocturne

1.

THE BALCONY OF OUR SIXTH FLOOR hotel room overlooks a courtyard around which several apartment blocks jostle for space. In most windows the lights are still on and doors leading to patios and balconies are open. We are two shadows, eavesdroppers, balancing our wine glasses on the concrete balustrade. Somewhere in the vast unruly city someone works the pedals of an out-of-tune parlour organ playing a cantata for many voices: children's cries, laughter, shouts, motorbikes, the siren's ear-piercing wails and the unruffled cooing of pigeons. From a steamed-up bathroom window comes the whine of a hair-dryer. Further to the right a woman raises her voice to a child who bursts into shrill sobs. Two dogs bark, a little high-pitched yapper and a deep hoarse slow-witted drawn-out woof-woof, an antiphon, point and counter point. Slowly the sobs are hushed, the child falls asleep; the hair-dryer is switched off; the barking ceases and the pedals rest. Lights go out except for one opposite high under the eaves. Below us the infernal blue flicker of a television continues until the rivers of the underworld rise and swallow it, wiping out bloodshed, deceit and comedy alike. And now the stars saunter through a gate which opens above us. In Haydn's *Farewell Symphony* the musicians rise, extinguish their candles and leave one by one until the stage lies in silence and darkness. The finale begins, a sleepy yelp, a shutter bangs, a man home late rattles his door keys. The rains of silence and darkness fall.

2.

THE FLYING BUTTRESSES of Banyan trees in the Botanical gardens, the otherworldly scent of citrus flowers, whole avenues of *bombax ceibas,* cotton wool spilling from the hard shells of their fruit like snow on the ground around them, others whose bulbous gun metal grey trunks bristle with iron-hard spikes. Each palm tree grown in rows along the shore of the Saracen Sea guards the sleep of a streetwise mongrel in its scanty shadow; this is the garden where dog deities rest after their day's work is done. We step onto a rough strand strewn all over with broken glass, washed in the sea's spinning cycle till it has become opaque and silken to the touch. The strand shines in the evening sun just as the endless Via Roma shines in the light of street lamps later that night. Wave after wave of pedestrians, carts, motorbikes, cars have swept over the black stone throughout the years and worn it smoother than the marble tiles of the city's crumbling palaces. This is the floor of abundance—we must kneel and take off our shoes to begin the ascent to our starred destination.

In the mornings always start with the sea

enter its glass vaults as it sways
and lifts its body towards the light

hungry for land and cliff
a fine dividing line inked

on the margins of its breviary,
blue washes on blotting paper.

But it is kind to swimmers, divers,
five-fingered stars, the salt skin of dreamers,

at noon there is something dance-like
in its movements, it

obeys a wavering
beat, febrile, restive, sifts

through edges, opens wide,
inhales the sun with grape-black mouth.

Listen for music in its depths:
the drawn-out dawn-lit stanzas

of seal song and whale call spilling,
echoing across a wide dance floor.

Go true south, press your ear to 30 feet of ice
to hear the choirs of the drowned sing.

Swifts

I can't believe they don't know what they're doing
that delight is unknown to them as they gather
preparing for the long and terrible journey.
It can't merely be all programme, hard-wire, protein,
plasma, synapse, cellular. They are too expert
at elevation and elation, those twin joys.
The other day I walked down a street
of small grey houses in my neighbourhood
and saw them take off and settle around a pole
from which five parallel wires were strung
to other poles, from those onto the eaves. There was
such excitement in the air, flutter
and twitter of a great activity, swing-up, dip
and vibrato of landing on the shakiest of landing strips,
their arrow-tailed dark bodies arranged on the
electric wires like quavers on a large grey sheet of music
I picked out and sang the melody they'd composed
in thirds and fifths, two Ds, three Gs, two Bs, and two more Ds,
then the whole gamut upped and modulated in one lift-off
to the top line F and with extravagant slurs
and glissandi flocked onto a nearby gutter.
A neighbour opening her door behind me said
they're gathering to say goodbye and will soon be away.
I sang the swifts' song to her then as best I could
but never mastered the mordents of farewell
as they slipped past us and beyond.

Dawn Chorus in Late April

TWO YOUNG SHANTALLAH MEN are painting the upstairs rooms. They sing together quietly while they work—*Moon River, Somewhere Over the Rainbow, When I'm 64*—sometimes they hum or one of them whistles. They dip their brushes into tins labelled Cirrus, Snow Drift, Sea Foam, Egret. As they fill fissures or smoothen over cracks in the old walls, the visionary light of orchards in blossom streams through the open windows. Once in the middle of rained-on Dublin traffic at near-standstill, in a bus crawling along the quays I heard a fine pure whistling behind me, tune after tune: *The Lark in the Clear Air, The Heather Breeze, The Blackbird,* and turning round I saw a small man in a dapper suit with steel-rimmed glasses. He sat upright gripping the metal support beside him, his feet in neat brown slip-ons didn't quite reach the ground. Later that night after wind and rain had taken themselves eastwards I stood at the window in a friend's house and looked out at a tall old beech. Somewhere in the thicket of its branches a bird sang. It was around one thirty in the morning but the bird sang. It sang of the night, it sang of house painters who break the glacial silence of walls, it sang of whistling champions on their way to collect their pensions in wet buses stuck in traffic, it sang of songbirds astray in foreign cities singing by the dawn light of street lamps and lit-up windows. As it sang, a door opened into a nocturnal garden where there was nothing but a tree rising up with illuminated boughs and leaves.

II

The Grass Garden

Gardens

Early morning. Someone played Scarlatti sonatas
in the house that lies in a granite garden by the sea.
The notes walked single file on air
waves and high wires strung between roofs,
a well-tempered procession.
Was it any wonder that within minutes
blackbirds and larks appeared to exchange tunes?

Later I went out thinking how for your entire life
you can carry the memory of a green garden
in your head and the memory
of a damnation in jade and blue mosaics,
and not know which is which.

Come down to the strand, the encounter
of sea and rock where all ideas
are twofold. Borderland. The idea of stone
and of water. Two pebbles plus two runlets
make one world. Look at us, say the boulders,
we shine, we glimmer, we are splendid,
imprinted with the orange, white and black
macula of lichen, the pale grey lichen
that prickles under your soles.
Clusters of sea pinks grow from hairline
cracks on us. A miracle. They lift
their tufted heads shivering and bowing
to the wind. Come into our garden and rest—

we are scoured, clean and silent.
What more could you wish for?

⁓

The last judgement in the golden-walled basilica on the island
is made of small pieces of glass tinted with the ink of moth wings,
of buttercups, matted hair, bone splinters, blue glass, owl
    feathers,
coal, sugar, pewter, bitumen, jelly fish, finger prints, gold leaf,
    mussel
shells, bat droppings, metal, umbilical blood, Chinese ink, fog,
black silk, haemoglobin, eel skin, touchstones, cuckoo flower
petals, glacial snow, saliva, sea water, granite and quartz.

⁓

The boats pulled up on Moyrus strand at low tide—
how empty they are,
wide open to surveillance from above—
the sun that peers at them through its scorching lens
and others, sharp-eyed, hungry
always on the cruise for scraps,
the rare salt grotesques left behind in the nets—

and how still they are now
where all was movement,
gesture, lilt and drift.

They have sunk so deep into pale wet sand
their names can't be read. Were it not
for mooring ropes and anchors
hooked to the rocks, we might all slip fast
from this measured and rooted world.

Sink or swim! says the sea, repeating its old
ultimatum and tugs at a portal in its depth
to let the iridescent shoals flit
from dark exits.

Awash with light, the boats wait
in the morning's spot-lit auditorium
where a herring gull stands
on a draughty rostrum lecturing
on the idea of flight.

We, too, wait to be lifted, for the wind
to leaf through the next pages
of our narratives,
to be called by name and given back
to flux—the luminous wild passageways.

Achill Killeen

for John and Ursula

1.
Early morning.
The holiday cottages across the bay are tired
from rowing all night through the surf
and lay their oars aside.

Far out between two rocks, the sun
opens a blue door
and ushers a trawler and crew into
the glittering high rise of the day.

2.
A tortoiseshell butterfly leads me
to where the waves unravel
all over the sand.

It is a scrap of the lost map
of the island blown here and there
with its browns wings
and delicate black delineations.

3.
I stand in a field above the sea
strewn with pieces
of white quartz
each marking a child's grave.

The stones are bright lamps lifted
out from the earth and placed
on a makeshift altar:

the old gods have come down
from the mountains
to watch over the field in pity and silence.

4.
The children had slipped out of reach
and into the earth so fast
their names were not written on stone.

But the young parents who knelt
on the hillside knew them by heart—
grief they were called, loss and anguish.

5.
All day a mild wind rakes the grass
and the clouds rush their cargo
of birds eastwards.

All day my feet go
here and there—all day my heart
wants to stand still.

Bonfire Weeds

for Miriam and Benjamin

> *Anyone who has made a bonfire in a field knows
> that for a long time only nettles and thistles will thrive
> where the grass roots have been scorched.*
> —Hubert Butler

Where they had carried the pallets, piled
them high on the waste
land near Skegoneill
between Victoria Gardens
and Glantrasna Drive, placed

the Others' flag on top, soaked it all with kerosene
and thrown in
a match

the fire rose and blossomed for a night
and day and finally
its red petals withering away
it lay down on the hot
earth, dark
and dead.

Then rain came cooling the soil
in which the seeds
already stirred
beneath charred
bits of wood,
blackened nails
debris and dirt,

then sun and more rain
and after a time
green shoots appeared and spread—
nettle, chick weed,
speedwell, thistle, henbane,
groundsel, dandelion—

common weeds
sprung from rough
ground and ash,
secretive and tough.

Stendhal Syndrome

for Miriam

We carried the sloe berries we had picked
along the marshland on Lough Erne,
its grassy verge dense with thorn scrub,

holly, young oak, birch, where sloe bushes grow
leggier than their stunted Connemara kin,
gathered them in hats, pockets, uplifted

skirt hems, leaving the top branches laden for the birds,
brought them into the kitchen—a harvest of sloes,
bluer than violent bruises and as hard as beads,

near coal-black but with an ash-grey flush
and the matte finish of fine suede,
each berry filled with an acidic drop of night,

and dropped them, sloe by pin-pricked sloe
into glass bottles up to half their measure,
decanted the clear liquor into them, topped them up

and finally funnelled the right quantity
of sugar to the brim, gave them a shake
and left them standing on the window sill for weeks.

The young artist to whom this offering was made
watched day by day the berries bleed
their cores into the alcohol, a gradual change take place,

the limpid medium turn colour caused by the union
of bitter fruit and sugar in the gin, a maculate conception
as in a chemical experiment, a stain that rose up

from the sloes, clear and deep red as garnets, and sampling it
she tasted meadows in the summer heat, saw green-scummed
   ponds
and a wide stretch of bog whose reeds, ignited by the sun

pouring its heart into the acid land, shone a pure yellow,
hence its local name the Golden Bog, where earlier, she told me,
driving past, a sudden dizziness and racing pulse

had made her stop the car and catch her breath—
not an artist's image of the world, she said, but the world itself,
its splendour, incomprehensible, dazzling, had swept her

with feelings of delight and longing, joy and loss at once,
and as she drank, she tasted leaf and root, fruit and decay,
the sweetness of the earth, as freely given as withheld.

The Grass Garden

OFTEN THE HEART ATTACHES ITSELF to the most insignificant of places. Great cities with wide teeming squares and fountains that fling water back to the clouds, steep cathedrals and the skyward thrust of their flying buttresses, the deep glass canyons and mazes of their streets—I admire them and yearn to lose myself on boulevards and markets, but their broken, mournful splendour overawes and terrifies the heart. The heart can not prefer nor select, it has no choice. It belongs in the earliest places where the imagination roamed and all the senses were engaged by solemn and unremarkable scenes, where objects and sensations cohabit inseparably and which we yearn to return to. It can take a whole lifetime to recognise this longing as something more than nostalgia—as a memory of irretrievable happiness, of once having been at one with things:

The sun-heated rough grain of the shed door under my hand. I pushed it open on an interior silvered with dust and cobwebs, secretive and odorous, something metallic and sharp mingled with the dark warm smell of ferment and decay. I entered the shed feeling a presence, that something marvellous lived in this nest-like space woven of needles of light from glinting surfaces—from the teeth of rakes, from shovels, blades, tins—and particles of sawdust, dead insects, motes, crumbling earth, dried weeds, the still hot air chock-full with mystery.

Outside green ruled; it welled up from uncut grasses between the fruit trees and from the strong bitter aroma of the box hedges around beds of herbs and nasturtiums in the vegetable garden. This scent was the deep, almost blue green of the garden seats under the trellised vines. We played there in the flickering light that filtered through dense foliage. In tree shadow our bare arms and legs were washed in a leafy wash, jade-coloured shadows lay under my brother's eyes and in the hollows of his cheeks, our palms were golden with pollen.

Spiders and beetles marched up the stems of grasses clad in lime green like gendarmes. On early mornings, the grass garden was sprinkled with dew drops refracting the light in their small prisms, and an upside-down world rolled to earth with each droplet if we brushed and shook the grass walking to the place where linen sheets were spread out to bleach in the sun. Daisies and buttercups wove a dense white and yellow fabric all over the lawn and caressed and cooled the soles of our feet.

The shutters were closed against the heat on summer days and to keep out killer wasps whose glistening angry hum we feared. Through the shutters the light cast parallel lines across the floor. I crawled to my favourite spot beneath the grand piano and watched my father's feet in polished black shoes press the pedals as he played. After a while they turned into two strange creatures, solitary twins dancing along with the music. The piano was open and, as his hands flitted over the keyboard, I climbed a stool to see the hammers, rows of miniature wooden men with felt hats, rhythmically touch the strings. The lid was hoisted high, the piano was an elegant black sailing vessel that took my father and me across the eddies and swirls of a dangerous current.

In the Garden of Images

IN THE GARDEN OF IMAGES I was sibling of the Good Grey Sister, the crooked old pear tree with its silvery-grey bark, I was daughter of the wolf who crept through the orchard and frightened me in my Sunday dress. Inside the house I belonged to the zinc bath in the kitchen und the mad girl stomping up and down the stairs. In the garden of images I was snail among snails in the corner by the well and the smell of the box hedge. Words opened their warm brown and mossy blossoms. My grandmother gave me a green drink made from wild mint and told me stories of poppies, of the small people that inhabited the flowering anise. Field mice peeped from burrows along the embankment and greeted us on the way to the lily valleys. When my brother fell into the well I was taken out of the garden, my mother gave me black silk ribbons for my hair and I cried at the funeral.

    I knew about Satan early, if I was good he would do what I wished; my brother had told me so. Outside the garden wall wild boars roamed the beech woods and a large black bird settled on the gate at dusk, his yellow eye focused on me. A boar was shot, slaughtered and hanged from the beech tree by the bridge. Its snout touched the dust of road. It was disembowelled and the skin inside the hollowed-out carcass was stretched tight over the bones and glistened like grandmother's opal brooch. Three wasps wandered slowly up and down the spine in the carcass. The evening bell rang and rang and my head carried my mother's head in church, we were pre-Columbian, two in one, a warm creature breathed behind me, pressed against my back and kept me safe. I felt the weight of her sleeping head on mine. Red tears as large as raspberries rolled down the face of the man who suffered for me. The pain had stiffened the blue wriggling veins along his thighs and torn his mouth open. My father's face appeared in a spiky silver mandorla and his voice sounded like warm velvet, different from the wolf voice in the garden.

There was always washing and ironing to be done in the kitchen, starch and bleach. On slaughter days the neighbours brought fresh meat dripping with blood, kidneys, sausages and hot round cakes cooked in lard. These were the nights of sleepwalking, of night-mares galloping through my dreams. And later there was vocabulary on lined pages, exercise books, dog-eared in leather satchels, the rules of syntax as my mother ironed and starched. The toughest words came much later: *conquest, general, equation, trigonometry, gravity, elegy, pluperfect, aorist, psychopathology.*

The Garden at the Road's End

Turn left at the elm with the heron's nest,
go past the Forbidden Village sign,
then right where the two thieves on the cross hide
under mounds of mildewed brambles,
take the long and narrow path for a mile or two
till you come to the garden at the road's end.
Three magpies, those bêtes noirs in their chalk
and ink plumage will spy you first,
cackle and mock you, trotting around on the grass
over flinders of eggshells—relics of a recent
murderous foray—then flap onto the thatch
for a better view. A wren seizing his chance
will speed into the white thorn hedge.
The sun will stare through the spokes of an old motorbike
parked in the yard, nettles and dandelions open
green telegrams beneath the trees that stand
in a circle around the house, stiff and tight
as police cordons. Silence and absence.
Go up close. Your heart in your mouth.
Pressing your ear against the door, listen
to spiders glide across the black and white
piano keys, the hammers softly touch the strings,
the pedals—or somebody's breathing—rise and fall,
the wind play funeral marches on a minor scale.

The Morning After

for Gabriel

All night the storm went on and on
it sang in the gullies
rode on our young birch trees
bending them to the ground,

it laboured and breathed noisily
trying to shift the mountains across the bay,
it threw itself headlong against
our door demanding to be let in.

Stay outside, storm, we said, give us
some peace, it is May and we want
our trees to grow straight and
the flowers we planted
to lift their heads to the sun.

But the storm continued its racket, it clattered
on the roof, threw
slates around, banged the gate shut
and finally emptied a hornets' nest
down our chimney.

In the morning the rain had washed
the colours off everything, the trees
stood with broken limbs.
Salt fire had scorched the young leaves
and burnt the blossoms

and all along the street the old
election posters flapped on the poles
and made a sad cacophony of
shattered promises and long faces.

Jardin Botanico

Let all city gardens be small like this one,
let them be dusty, enclosed
by a wrought-iron fence
painted peacock-blue,

the gates pockmarked with rust,
a waiting room for the physicians of silence
in the heart of the teeming city below
the Sierras.

Ibn al-Baytar strolled through the jardin
in 1225 with his notebook
of Andalusian flora, picking
the odd flower to sniff its bouquet

or crushing a leaf, then solemnly
added descriptions: species
and healing properties of *nigella damascena*
or *lavandula angustifolia*—Arabic minuscules

in brown ink on parchment, the script marching
from right to left. Not many come here now.
I wander in the bright and dark-green
cross-hatched scents of childhood

through rivers, avalanches of light and heat.
Above me the mountains open their stone
portals on snow drifts and glaciers. Legend
has it that men set out from here in winter

to climb the peaks and returned
weeks later, snow-blinded but with
calm souls carrying ice-sealed jugs.
Anise and rosemary grow through the box hedge,

flower beds wear tattered hems
fringed with aromatic prickly grasses,
a yellow dust lies in the air.
Let this be a refuge for snow gatherers

and cloud hunters, here they can lie
under the trees and listen to water
course through the tall mimosas, through roots,
trunks and boughs into the finest

capillaries of their feather-tipped twigs,
watch pine branches shake out dark
Moorish tent fabrics, hear cicadas
work on their enduring minimalist score,

the gingko leaves play
a two-fingered music older than gardens,
the moon toll its bell
suspended from the eaves of night.

Chinese Garden

> *Everything has beauty but not all can see it*
> —Confucius

1

By the Portal to Wisdom
the words of Confucius, teacher of humanity,
graven into mossy black stone
are loudly mocked by the cuckoo.

A tortoise crawls
from under the snow lantern
on the summer pond island,
ambles to the edge and plunges in:

back leg kicking,
head held high above water—
the fastest swimmer in this garden.

Swallows and dragonflies
distribute their news bulletins, zig-
zagging over the surface.

The silver poplar's quivering breath
mingles with the complete
stillness of blue.

An airplane passes the curled shaving
of a day moon—
origami bird
trailing a feather of white smoke.

Inside a green tunnel of plane trees
shadow light—
pulsating rose—
closes and opens the soul's chambers.

2

Above a cloud of umbrellas
I see the rain bird
rise up swift as an arrow.

A crane winds his long neck around
one knee joint and stares
into the cosmos of its claws.

Rain-lacquered trees spread
their three- to four-fingered leaves
over the woodcutter's cottage.

Dripping wet, a monk
hurries past
concealing something under his cloak—

I'd like to know—a scroll
or his heart?
In any case: blood-red, blood-hot.

III

Travelling with Ruby

The poet at eighty takes out the 17 colours

for Pearse Hutchinson on his 80th birthday

of water and paints a winding road by the sea
a blue-slated house with a narrow green
staircase and a window sill on which two apples
and three oranges lavish
their scent on the world, he paints
a door that leads into a tree at the back of the garden
a door into a stone wall, a door into the sea—
all are wide open—he paints
the liturgy of the wind near a lake and the reeds'
murmured response, he paints
a few boys playing in a field as the light throws
its arms around them, he paints
the hoof beats of a brown foal
on a Gloucestershire meadow, he paints
the most beautiful word in Russian, he paints
the violated body of the synagogue, he paints
his own heart which never ages
returned from the sun-lit canals of Haarlem
from nights in the garden of longing
the garden of revelry,
its tremor sets the glasses a-tinkle on his table, he paints
the strange wild melodies of Cataluña, he paints
books in which words lie asleep
curled around their own shadows, others
that rise from the pages and stream into the world
with the rustle of silk, he paints
bookshelves, paintings, photographs filled
with their familiar strangeness,
and finally himself seated in his chair

his hands resting in his lap
his hands that help to straighten out
the world's disarray with tenderness
and a tidy elegant script.

Homage

The poet feels light-hearted in her house by the sea—
now that she is almost ninety she can say
that all ill spirits, despair, guilt, regret have long fled
her threshold and are engaged elsewhere.

She only remembers now if and what she wants—the honeyed
    light
of late summers, winter winds, salty and brazen, the healing
    bitterness
of poems, stars slipping down August dawns, and most of all
she loves the spectacle just outside her windows

performed daily in her honour: the maritime birds
whizzing back and forth on their trapezes, the dizzy
stunts of the tides and the way the storm conjures
a polished coin from a pocket of rain clouds at night.

Blackberry lanes wind downhill to the last spit of land
where she lives alone in a house with a blue door
and the sea comes and goes freely
high up over White Beach.

It's the home of music and courtesy, safeguarded
for the moment by her non-judgmental cat since the poet
has just gone out to her trampoline and now flies high
with a breeze from Ben Bulben caught in her wild grey locks.

From a height she sees the whole bay ringed by the glistening
horizon, a friend's cottage and himself at his keyboard as he writes
his scorching, witty lines, she sees her children
and grandchildren at different ends of the earth,

she sees islands setting out like ships from their ports
and fields like green baize tables in libraries, and all she sees
and her books freed from the shelves sail the air with her—
>   *Hope against Hope*
in dark times, also Baudelaire the flâneur's perfumed volumes,

all the women saints, and one by one her old lovers, husbands
>   and friends,
as well as countless noble beasts of the wilderness
join her, tigers in amber and black, proud lions
and panthers, shining as liquid tar.

They surround her to tell her their stories, dreams and
terrors and joys above dust, ashes and pain,
elevated by the scent of wild flowers,
upheld by the silent earth's golden white light.

The poet at ninety writes a letter

for Stella Rotenberg

My friends, here at this table
with pen and paper
I want to tell you what I lost
which was everything
and what has in time returned to me
which also was everything.

As a child in the days of summer I learned
from my mother the language of stories
she taught me the poetry of sun
and bird, of leaf and grass
she taught me their green stanzas and
the epics of river and forest
she taught me the alphabet
of the rain that wrote on everything.

When I grew up
my mother's language
was thrown stones
to feed on and dead earth.
In exile it spoke: *jug   bowl   bread*
nothing else stood on my table.

And yet in darkness and sorrow
I put on a young girl's dress.
I opened a gate called *blossom*
a gate called *star*
a gate called *wave*
through each I passed with my
beating heart and saw
my mother on a veranda of summer light.

You must believe me
all I ever wanted
was for *bread and growth to flourish*
that the blood of the flower
would be stilled

to teach myself and you
to beware of despair

Evening near Letterfrack

I'd brought the papers into the house, the saddest
stories for years, newsprint wet from rain or was it tears
blackened my hands and now I watched the mountains—
old herd of nags—lower themselves around the bay,
hippodrome-style. The sky was clearing, islands reappeared.
Clare Island, Bofin, Inishturk and way out High Island
seesawed among the breakers. Fast forward breezes
shook quaking grass, sorrel, colt's foot, rhododendrons,
fuchsia shrubs, the rustling of some broad-leafed bush
sounded as if a score of blades were being sharpened.
Out near the strand a rock, a fossilized cetacean
was inch by inch submerging in the rising tide.
A feather of a cloud in the sheer sky withstood
the inroads of two transatlantic vapour trails
for longer than two minutes. Dog bark and pheasant call,
a donkey heehawed like a rusty barn door hinge
and on the trade routes of the birds
the evening traffic went on, swift and purposeful.
Such clarity of air, voices were carried far across
from a sandy beach beside the pier. Two women
walked the tidemark together in complete intimacy
picking up flotsam, stones and shells, the keepsakes
of a day they wanted to remember.
The one, young, black, wore a Nubian crown
of plaited locks, the other's head shone in the evening light
like weathered driftwood, smooth, bleached and silvered.
They talked as friend to friend, mother to daughter,
old to young, black to white. Two dogs were chasing
one another around them in the tidal surf.
Where were divisions now? The line between
the water and the sky, all binaries and opposites

dissolved here at the end of Europe
among the quartzite stones and soft black bog.
Don't be afraid, someone sang in the distance,
and, *I'll stay with you!*
The air was brimful of avowals and annunciations.

Four People on a Lake

Three hundred and sixty-five volcanic islands scattered
along the shore of Lake Nicaragua, each
with barely enough room for one house.

No human is an island perhaps, but each of these isletas
possessed a soul behind fringes of bougainvillea
and tropical green.

There was a small church on one, it glinted
in the sun, just discernible
between tree tops,

on another a school, a corrugated roof
on a few posts where wisdom could
come and go as it pleased,

on a steep rock in splendid isolation a villa—the flag
of the most powerful nation rose stiffly
in the breeze above it—

and on an island with a landing pier of rough planks
tables were set offering food and drink
in the shade of a mango tree.

Our boat glided along narrow channels through
the reeds. We sat in silence, four people
from four different countries.

White herons stood sentry-still, in the shallows.
Forgotten were sleepless nights, regrets,
worries, heart-ache.

A jewelled bird swayed on a branch, water lilies
dallied in yellow birthday hats, sea lettuce
was everywhere, rootless, adrift

on the glittering surface. The Danish woman stared
through the lens of her camera, unable
to believe her own eyes.

The young boatman who ferried us asked her politely
to post her photograph of him
to the second last house

before the old jacaranda on the León road. All this time
islands, boatman, ourselves and all else on the lake
the lake itself and all its creatures

the trees, plantations, fields and deserts around it, the far-away
coasts of two oceans, dusky cordilleras, cloud forests,
volcanoes beneath smoke rings

farms, villages, cities, people and animals were
held in the dispassionate gaze of a pair
of maritime eagles that circled

and cruised overhead, air-lifted by the thermals
into a blue way beyond
our mortal vision.

The Spider Revisited

1.

The spider that scuttled across the bathroom last night
was still there today struggling up the side
of the tub. I watched it lose its foothold, try to haul
itself up, slither down the enameled slide
and plunge back into the void.
I wondered should I play god,

and lifted it onto the ledge of the bath
with the handle of a brush. It slipped back
dangling and circling mid-air for a while
at the end of its invisible tether, a nest
of spikes, tangled darkness and dust,
so I blew on it—a soft breath—

it spun around, abseiling unspooled
ten or fifteen inches of silk,
and wriggled free to reel
itself in again. God must feel
misunderstood like that, I thought;
then I recalled heads of state and their ilk,

the countless examples of human folly, and abandoned
the spider, hanging in white
emptiness with nothing to delight or thrill
its greedy sinister heart, shut
the door on it as a god might
have, bored, cranky, sad.

2.

You wanted to play god? So I tricked you
by playing helpless. Yet a hundred eyes
on my back kept you in sight. I smelled
you even before I saw you:
the usual oily mixture

of the disgust and fascination I inspire
preceded you. Had you overcome your fear
and lifted me, held me in the hol-
low of your hand, your palm
and fingers could not have enclosed me.

I am too long-legged, fashioned by genius
perfectly centred, seesawing on eight
points of the compass in my spiral
orb. I am a divinity in the halls
of my own worship, an idol, elegant,

poised on the tables of my mathematical
dining rooms of grace, my latticed larders,
you're a boorish, shadowy, unwel-
come presence in this spot-lit space
of sinks, pipes, unsavoury smells.

Let me warn you, I have a skill
the goddess bestowed on me alone of all
creatures: I am gifted, I reveal
the hidden vices of the gods
woven into my flimsiest webs, visible to all.

Feeding Time

for Ruby, Lesy, Clea and Julian

It's not the simulated wave behind glass
        that thunders every three minutes
                against the rocks

nor the conger eel, dark lord of drain pipes
        and sea caverns, not even
                the saw teeth

of the starry smooth hound
        on its restless back and forth glide
                that can detain the children

but pulling us fast by the hand
        they stop to linger, point, call out
                at a round shallow basin

where they would see them
        as a bird or a god might see them
                from a height

in their shadowy universe
        where the earth and all its creatures
                are flat

and everything is buoyancy, silence
        and circular, glass-
                sealed horizons:

    schools of plaice grown huge in captivity
        speckled discs, dim moons
            that orbit indolently

    or rays, kite-tailed, more intricately patterned
        than the most fanciful
            Japanese fabric

    the fluid stroke and flap of their wing-like fins
        that glint in the milky underwater light
            as tin foil might

    trimmed with fine copper wire trim around
        the rippling edges, adrift and cruising
            on their otherworldly cruise,

    flashing the odd Morse message
        with tiny tinsel-backed mirrors that go on
            and off on their languid bodies.

    At feeding time they rise in a twinkling, lift
        blunt heads, ogle lop-sidedly from the water
            mouths agape as if they wished

    to have a word with the young man in blue overalls
        whose offering—an iridescent dollop
            of hake—they accept

    without as much as a blink of close-set eyes
        then one toss of their pelerines
            and they sashay

back into their universe, singularly aloof
    bewitching and more
        fine-grained

than the pale sand on the ground
    with which they blend
        so seamlessly.

There is no hope on earth for us
    they might reveal the measure
        of their insight.

But the children, the bravest first,
    slip their hands into the basin.
        They touch the fish

they feel the skin of a poem composed by fish
    rough as sandpaper or cool
        and slippery as silk

with their fingers and something—
    a memory from long ago—surfaces
        and touches them:

weightlessness
    shadow world
        well-spring.

Travelling with Ruby

Seven a.m. The rain clouds of the West
have conspired to pour
their damp hearts out just on our
heads as we approach the railway station with

its one-track mind and its one track East,
the distant places we are bound for.
On the platform a queue of travellers more
sleeping than awake inch snail-like past

huge lettering in white on blue
that reassures us Jesus loves you too .
No shred of doubt that this is so
in the minds of two nuns near us in the queue,

with their sheer black plastic rain coats
and black dripping cases the nuns
look like benign cormorants.
Ruby asks questions, her hand in mine is hot.

A princely Irish-African punches our tickets.
She pulls her red Charlie and Lola bag.
asking Why are donkeys always sad?
We settle down, Ruby unpacks

covers the table with toys, markers, playing
cards, a tiny golden cup, a special treat
for later. Was there always air? will it run out?
The train sets off across the railway bridge,

on the wrinkled skin of Lough Atalia
below us sail two miniature swans
as though adrift on grey crêpe de chine
then gorse, rocks, inlets, a single white horse.

Here come the famous fields of Athenry
checkerboard-straight, grasshopper green
the greenest shade you've ever seen.
Ruby draws an elephant with twenty toes.

The country's longest garden lies in a ditch
from west to east along the railway line:
Woodlawn, silver birch, weeping birch, pine
horsetail, loosestrife, purple vetch.

Speedwell, sings the engine, speedwell,
sloe bush, reply the wheels, sloe bush, sedge
no one can buy the garden in the ditch,
melancholy thistle, holy grass, pennyroyal, not for sale.

Stonewalls, horses, sheep, more horses, countless sheep
lambs play tig round alders in a circle on a hill,
hundred-year-old sleepers asleep in a pile.
We feast on crisps. *Do elephants stand when they sleep?*

Wetlands, river banks, high water, floating trees,
the cows are wading through the flood
up to their udders. And now a neat
well-varnished station house, ivy-clad, crows—

gone again. Just glimpsed: a halting site, pie-
balds, white plastic garden chairs like sentries
beside a water tower, redbrick chimneys
in serried ranks out of the corner of the eye.

We play Jack-change-it. Ruby nearly always wins.
Stopped in the middle of nowhere
the sun crawls from its den at last, its lion's fur
shines dandelion-yellow, blackbird song and wrens.

Almost there now; houses, hedges, streets, more streets …
Ruby's asleep. A floral mixum-gatherum
of scarlet begonias, daisies, geraniums
planted in tractor tyres painted white

at the next station. Such abundance, a windfall
of gardens in backyards, on platforms,
wilderness gardens along railway lines. We slow down
in a light-filled hall, the doors open. Arrival.

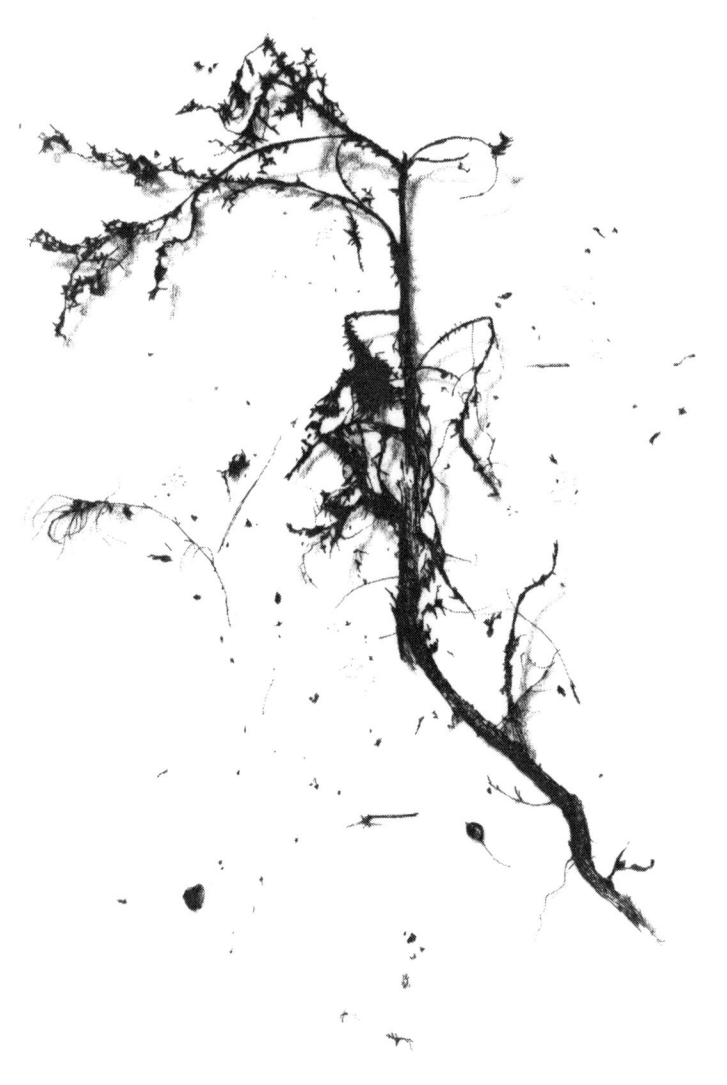

IV

The Heart of Things

Notes from Henry Street

with apologies to Montale

I

Gales that played wild and loose all night
with rubbish in the street and flung plastic
forks like confetti round the garden have died
away to the hum of Astras and Toyotas on wet tarmac.
There are worm-eaten floorboards in my room
and from the kitchen comes the smell of burning
toast. Non-stop rain blows in from the sea
along our street of Club Paradiso, sex shop
plus blackjack club, drifts past FOR SALE signs, past
the latest apartment block's rain-blackened walls,
silvering my window with salt,
and I write to you from this remote table,
the cubicle, the satellite thrown into space—
and the silent TV, the fireplace
with its dusting of ashes, the veins
of slug slime and mould are the setting
which soon you will be coming home
to. These days, as I consider the narrative
of my life, are full of bluster and no chance
of an escape to gentler zones in sight.
Your photo's on my wall—your smile lights
up my room. It's raining hard from here to Finisterre.

II

Dear poet, we have no courtyards here, no fountains
scaling lofty architectural heights, but Texaco
stations, investment premises, condominiums,
shoddy, double-glazed, shuttered. Below
a platoon of gulls—sizeable monsters—en route to gutters,
eaves, the nocturnal streets brightly lit as day,
Midnight is noughts and dashes on a digital display.
We have screen-tested Andromeda—thin patterns
of stars that spiral round a vacuum—via satellite.
Memories return nocturnally, sere and raw. Ivy
spreads on partition walls, a dark bitter smell. Tonight,
my footsteps resounding on the pavement,
I wish, as you then did, for gales to return, northerly
and more savage than before, to lash through narrow lanes
sweep clear the hopeful, uncertain mind.
What can I say to the war reports, the endless
drip from black drains? Lights expire flickering,
the mountains across the bay, a critical mass,
lie compacted and black, the wind's bickering
as ever, time trickling down the glass.
Instead, I have words with the dead, with death
with death who is alive and well and kicking.

Last Seen

Again today in our local shop a poster:
an A4 Xeroxed photo of a young man
of twenty who's missing since the weekend, lost or

maybe worse. So often and so like each other
the young faces, something about the eyes ... Again
today taped to the poles in Henry Street this poster.

Who wrote *Last seen late Friday night?* The sister
who knew he'd worn grey hoody, jeans and tan
boots, left the club around two? Since lost or

feared worse. Please, urgently contact his father,
if he's been spotted near the river, anyone
who may recall his face having seen the poster?

A diligent economics student in his last year,
quiet, polite and popular with everyone.
His mother's worried unto death he's lost or

worse—gone where she cannot reach him, where
the saddest keepsake she'll have of her son
is an A4-size Xeroxed missing person's poster,
a never-answered question that will haunt her.

MIDNIGHT—A DOCUMENTARY about street kids in Gambon. The camera as instrument in the uncovering and putting on record. The children lie still, emaciated bodies, stick legs, long narrow feet, about a dozen of them, hard to say how old they are, between six and fourteen perhaps. The camera stays on their faces, they return the gaze, for a whole minute or more, expressionless, neither lowering their lids nor blinking—then nervous twitches, jerking movements of the hands, arms flung out to rummage beneath rags for the bottle with the solution, they pour the substance from the bottle into their palms, rub them together and sniff from the hollow of their hands; after a few seconds they keel over and lie still. This scene is repeated over and over, on the margin of the cities, next to piles of rubbish, stinking sewage culverts. If a grown-up comes across them they are cursed and beaten away like mangy dogs. The lens of the camera is almost constantly directed at their faces—their features show little life, sometimes, they bare their teeth, revealing many gaps, their eyes roll back, they mumble—then the camera moves around and across their heaped bodies, legs covered in sores. The subtitle repeated over and over reads *Où sont les enfants?*

Orplid

> *Du bist Orplid, mein Land, das ferne leuchtet*
> —Eduard Mörike

The river had shrunk to a trickle when we returned,
cities to chessboard size; years later
the house, the childhood rooms were dwarfed,
the garden displayed what you
had never seen: crippled leaves, heaped dust

poor blighted boundary hedges, still
in spring leaves push from deep red casings
and trees stand caught in a time lapse
inside glittering nettings of March
showers. The proud prickly gorse

bursts into yellow abundance as ever,
each blossom a masterpiece of medieval
deftness, the same chorus of bees
burrows into vanilla scents.
The communality of grass and moss spreads

over gravel and damp soil.
How it begins anew and continues,
the branches perpetually move to an inner rhythm,
back-gardens, blackbird song, garden furniture—
the rusted swings that bring tears to your eyes,

the hooked letter stamped in our passports
the star stitched to our hearts

The Heart of Things

I. Journey

At the station, newspapers, hot
coffees, the metallic smell of departure, the larks
strike their notes, glitzy
overtones from on high after night rain.
The train carries us away free
of hesitation or doubt on its linear tracks.
Fleecy clouds move with us, fast
fleeting farewells.
Approaching the heart of things equals becoming
the heart of things, I read green
hierograms of birches, leaf music,
shiver light, breathing.
On each page I turn, small shadows rush
across the script, glass-winged
as dragonflies, unburdened of all else.
The boy next to us, seventeen maybe eighteen,
is asleep, his head on his folded arms,
on the table beside him his cap, phone,
glasses, wallet, all given over
to happenstance, the touch
of sunlight on his unburdened eyelids.

II. The Walk-In Heart

In the Trans-Alpine struggling uphill to Brennero
our compartment door kept sliding open
and shut again with a small click: the day outside
had trained its wide-angle lens on us.

A snow-covered book lay open beyond the windows
into which conifers printed their names, a cuneiform text
as far as the timber line. From three chimneys
smoke rose into the sky scrolled as the hems
of saintly garments—a threefold assumption.

In the strip show of mirrors above our seats
peaks swung round and orbited away from us,
viaducts receded on stilts,
lakes lay still under the greenish sheen of marble.

I was neither here nor there, felt as though
a strange language was drifting through me. Each word
weighed less than a breath. The engine pounded
and pounded as it climbed higher as though aspiring
to gain on some unquestionable transcendence.

It was as set on its purpose as the heart
in a Chicago museum inside which
I had stood and listened a long time ago.

At the last stop before dark
border guards verified us. The night rose
slowly like water. We speeded downhill
past platforms with unspellable names. Towns
spread their brocaded ribbons across the plain,
glimmered and dissolved in a bowl
full of blackness.

III. Global Economy

The train made strides on fiery tracks.
Second stop: a melancholy Woodlawn
weeping birches
the somber organization of spruce.

Low-slung clouds in tune with the withered
brown discolorations of heather and bracken,
flocks of starlings flung themselves into the sky
blacker than grape shot.

In the day's paper I read
of two young Chinese lovers, murdered
carried together from their Belfast apartment.

I wanted to get off and lie down
on the spinning planet
hold close to me the round-faced girl
the lanky boy in his college-logo T-shirt.

Who invents the stories we have to live
until the final sentence?

The train sliced through the countryside
the murderous narrative—
the yielding open heart.

IV. Tempest

We sped into complete darkness,
only the gigantic birds of lightning flew
trembling ahead of us
through the black sky.

Suddenly the clouds opened up
on a world stage back-lit by slanting
falling gold and the prompter's voice
repeated over the intercom

we ask the travellers' forgiveness
we ask the travellers' forgiveness.
When rain drops hit the window panes
our mirrored faces were awash with tears.

As if mid-tilt

Galway-Dublin train

Not even Tiger Ireland deserves the gall
of the man in the brown Truman Capote suit,
dickey-bowed and waist-coated, who falls

onto the worn plush of his seat and pulls
his hat over his face when the shrill cry
of a baby somewhere in the carriage calls

him from half-dreamt schemes of glory;
so he glares in the direction of the small
offender, shouts into his phone in bad German,

but the crying continues, elemental,
wild, despairing—although the mother tries
to hush it, it's beyond consolation, all-

encompassing, a high-pitched lament
that engulfs everything in its sorrow:
mother, overcast evening sky, the end

of another day, the trees we pass, single-
minded in their flicker-shadow
dance, the two women across the aisle

who reminisce about Lourdes, *the hotel
staff so negligent, so rude,* the gentle Polish girl,
bringer of coffees and brave smiles,

until the whole world weeps, the spring rain
streaking the window panes, all
of us as we sit here; I think of a friend

with heavy heart who was recalled
still far from the finishing line
as if mid-tilt, mid-air, amidst so much still

Stations

For years my father-in-law lived in silence at the heart of noise
traffic and movement, station master
of a tiny station on the line
where the Glasgow-London Express sped through
and just one train stopped daily

with a cargo of carrier pigeons.
Over time he'd load and unload
hundreds of cages full of tall graceful birds
who huddled together a little nervously
and peered at him with dark intelligent eyes.

Veterans of the war, decorated
with military medals, they had flown
thousands of miles, saved lives and never
lost their way. He took care not to upset them
when lifting the cages out. Banished

from home he had taken
the mail boat to just about anywhere—
never contacted his family.
One day one of his sons passed through
in the London-bound Express

and saw him sweeping the platform. His shout
startled the other passengers
but the train had rushed through the station.
Too poor for a radio he constructed one—
a magnet wound with wire to which he attached ear phones—

tuned into broadcasts on medium wave after work
from home and the world: Dublin, Hilversum, Prague, Helsinki.
He grew geraniums along the platform,
drank strong sweet tea in his ticket office
where no one bought a ticket to anywhere,

before returning to the men's hostel
where he slept. When he retired
there was a notice in the local paper:
Paddy Goes Home.
His name wasn't Paddy.

A History of Photography

1. BLACK AND WHITE

> *Photographs state the innocence, the vulnerability of lives heading towards their own destruction.*
> —Susan Sontag

Holding a square of paper, three by three
inches, darkened and cracked
with age—I see her as the photographer
must have seen her through
his all-seeing lens:
this four-year-old running
for dear life, still running after
a century today across the sunlit
cobbled street, in hand-knitted
stockings and floral
dress, running breathless
headlong almost blindly
a smile on her face
running to escape the two figures
in dark overcoats and hats
who stand at a distance and watch her
strive towards the bridge
the swing in the walnut tree, run
straight for the shadow that falls
at an acute angle across
the foreground, straight into
the next century with its as yet
unknown disasters and losses
If I could stop her
kneel down on the cobbles
to stop her with my arms
if only I could stop her with open arms

2. CLASS PHOTOGRAPH

> *According to Lichtenberg*
> *only very few people have ever seen a pure white.*
> —Ludwig Wittgenstein
>
> *In front of the photograph of my mother as a child, I tell myself: she is*
> *going to die: I shudder (…) over a catastrophe which has already occurred.*
> —Roland Barthes

Unfashionable hair styles, plaits, ringlets,
forty or more pale little faces,
fuzzy, overexposed. They stand
stiffly with folded hands.

Being photographed is a serious
affair. One must keep absolutely still. In 1918
no twittering bird escapes
from the black drapes of the machine.

The portrait of the emperor with handlebar moustache
and gala uniform hangs
above the blackboard. Mother, I found you again
centre of the third row

in your corona of light curls and your dress
with the lace collar. You link your friend,
and look straight at the camera, carefree
but a little in awe of the visitor with his box.

I'd know you anywhere, the hesitant smile
of the six year-old, the pure white
of the lace among the lightless greys
and blacks that overshadow the century.

3. Vertigo

> *There is no need for me to represent a body in order for me to experience this vertigo of time defeated.*
> —Roland Barthes

This city girl in tailored suit,
pillbox hat, pumps,
released from ten hours'
slave labour
leaps high
across
the moment, the rain,
the overflowing gullies,
the entire day.
Since morning she has been on a long slow
trajectory towards this leap
transforming all
that previously passed
into a second of flight,
and a heart-spinning
levitating gladness
as she leaps to meet
a lover
or the possibility of one
forever suspended
above the puddle and her own
capsized reflection.
All around her tall buildings
ablaze with neon
make the city streets seem
absurdly weighed down
with permanence
and a gravity

she has transfigured
into lightness
and I am dizzy
watching her.

4. Self-portrait, 1939

> *Whether or not the subject is already dead, every photograph is this catastrophe.*
> —Roland Barthes

Here's my self-portrait, shot on a bridge,
near Munich in 1940. See how I lean
on the parapet wearing a white dress.
The others went to see a view,
so I put the tripod at a distance, set up
the shutter release, posed and in the blink

of an eye I was caught inside
the light box. See how I squint
into the sun, how the wind tries
to lift my summer hat to blow it across
the Isar to the dark hills where conifers
climb the slopes. What happened next?

My hat tore loose eventually and whirled
past river, trees, hills—
and I myself was spirited away
by gradual silver halide erosion
and took my place among the forgotten.

And in the end?
Was it some lingering illness
that killed me or the darkroom toxins?
Or was I buried beneath the rubble
of Munich? I can't seem to remember.
Should I have watched the signs,

the rallies in the squares,
the marching songs, shouts, shots,
the birds scattering in a panic
from the tree tops on the left,

the ineradicable stain that spread
across the image from the margins
blotting out the world?

August Near Südstern

The sturdy gentleman outside
the Café Lux devours his meal, his dog
takes careful note of every bite.
The red and white umbrellas flog

high garden spirits, and the sunlight passes
through empty pools of mirrors in the bar,
each green-blue vein in cocktail glasses
a drunken streak. August, a shaggy beast,

sleeps stretched full-length beneath
dead leaves—they're this year's first—
and an unseasonal tristesse
creeps grey and cold among the trees

inching past couples in the shade,
until at last it settles down
next to a woman on her own
talking in whispers to herself who tries

recalling what she had known best
in all the years: the names and faces
of friends and lovers, the familiar places
so dear to her, all gone, all lost.

Elementary Poem

after W.G. Sebald

Lord, I was on my way one night recently, heading
in the direction of Munich, São Paolo, Shanghai,
Mexico City, it was not yet morning,
when I saw in the distance below me
something remarkable in the area of Berlin
The inner courtyards of apartment blocks
were lit up by a weak light, bluish, wavery
and then I saw it everywhere:
a blue glow streamed through window curtains
and blinds, unsteady, flickering as water.
Then it occurred to me: it was election
night and even in Marzahn behind curtains and blinds
the people were awake, hence the glimmer, thin
and trembling as glimmers of hope usually are.
And as I continued, I saw in the backyards
and rows of terraced houses all over the city
a muted effulgence: people were looking at their screens.
The pine forests of Brandenburg formed
a black fringe round the lakes in which
pinpoints of blue light were reflected and danced.
As I went on I saw it was election night
not only in Marzahn, but also in Steglitz
and Lichterfelde, Kreuzberg and Hermsdorf,
Friedrichshain, Tegel as well as Wedding.
A bluish pulsating garland
was slung round Berlin winding its way
along boulevards and through lanes.
I saw my acquaintance, the egyptologist in Dahlem
in its glow, the lady from the flowershop

in the Zossenerstrasse, the Celiks and all their
four children, Selim, Hatice, Mehmet
and Mustafa, the Tunisian wizards from the
computer shop, my Polish family doctor,
the beautiful waitress from the pizzeria,
the young woman from the check-out in Kaiser's.
From all their windows dimly flickering
lights seeped and spread like wild fire.
In the Marzahns of the whole earth was election
night, in the suburbs of Cleveland and Detroit as well
where people are forced to live in cars together with
their dogs, cats and budgies, wash
in gas station loos because their homes
were repossessed. The will-o'-the-wisp like
light shone everywhere, muted, iridescent.
The desperate tubercular glimmer of hope
illuminated the banks of Lake Victoria
where the fish are running out of air and
children pick the last shreds from maggoty
fish cadavers, piled high as hills and abandoned
by European exporters; where they boil
glue from the bones and sniff it to fly
far from their hopeless existence. I saw it
in Cairo glistering in the lanes of the old town
where bakers tip sawdust into the bread dough
because there's not enough flour for the poor,
in the sugar cane fields of Brazil, cultivated
for bio-fuel, that constantly swallow
more land driving the farmers from their
small homesteads; it was wherever agricultural
labourers are sprayed daily with pesticide
from helicopters, where families live on rubbish
tips and children in sweatshops sew
sports clothes or winter coats for global discount
stores in return for starvation wages.

In Managua I noticed the flicker in the favelas
in cardboard huts where ten-year-old boys sleep
who lug building blocks twelve hours a day
for one single dollar so they can feed
their small brothers and sisters, I saw it
where street kids are forced to be streetwalkers,
where girls and boys sell themselves
for a pittance to tourists. I saw it where people
live among the rubble of their bombed-out
houses in Lebanon and Gaza and it lit up
thousands of messages, written to you, Lord,
stuck into the crevices of the Wailing Wall
in Jerusalem. The cyanotic marvellous light
shone in the windows of my friends in Boston,
the entire East Coast of the US glittered
like an enormous fireworks display. The sea
was still rigid and black as cold lava but New England
lay beneath fringes of a celestial lustre.
Yes, perhaps it's too much to hope any human
could make the tiniest dent in the iron
progress of history. A human being is only
human, we all know that the hands
of even the best are tied and that the guillotine
of lies and self-interest hangs above every honest word.
But allow us this hope for a while
as you allow the dreamer
to pursue his dream to the end, and the poet
his vision of white roomy tents in the desert
and a radiant city that stretches along the
shore of the sea in front of the towering
snow peaks of Africa, of coasts full of sails
and rigging, tall ships, barges and boats.

V

Journal from the Mirrored Cities

Journal from the Mirrored Cities

WRITING WITH BOTH HANDS, an art that few master. In Leonardo's mirror script is doubled, reversed. The ambidextrous play with two hemispheres, air and water, words that fall off the margins to the left and right. Language doubles back, the fun, the encoding, mysterious and transparent. Two sisters write their own secret language in reverse. A young man declares his love back to front on the fender of his car driving the length and breadth of the city. The message blooms inside my cupped hands, petal upon petal. It flows through my hands sheerer than water.

SCRIPTORIUM OF THE PARK, secrecy, esoterics and power. Each leaf, twig, stone, bird, nest a sign, a cipher. A gathering of loafers and vagrants, all interlopers on the benches on spring mornings. We are eternal students, left-handed readers of nature, the body's proportions, the pale petals of an early crocus, the expressionism of trees, sounds, sighs, shouts, beetle tracks, the river's green current. On the scales lie magic spells and newspaper headlines, the lie, the short-lived word evaporates, the exact phrase rises like laughter or the pungent smoke from our cigarettes.

IN SOME NEWSPAPER SHOPS young women talk to themselves, they are wired up to speaking devices, oblivious to the girth of plane trees shedding their bark in spring. Once and for all they rewind and fast-forward the days of the week, hand me five years of change without batting an eyelid at my reflections. They are in possession. They win the day.

KAYAKING NOVICES IN streaming primary colours ease themselves off the bridge into the water. Leaving one medium for another they now are wound tightly, coiled and sprung. The kayakers rock in the Y of their palindromic crafts, flip over, agile as coots to attend the university of water plants, the sub-aqua perspective of swans, the wild eddies and swirls, the crowds on the markets, the currencies of today's business, whatever circulates fast, along main arteries and in and out of the heart of a city. How they cling to the bridges as the water levels rise. In vain, because, as Leonardo notes, in the vast forests huge numbers of trees are cut down.

THE HOUSES SWIM towards each other, drift apart on the water's shaky mirror, they have learned to keep afloat, to step in line, hold on and let go yielding to the undertow. All surfaces are scoured, the colours washed, weather-bleached, the wind has sanded down the quays to a fine mica glimmer. Driven into the swampy underground, a dark army in serried ranks, a forest of wooden posts, a consolidated nothing. Below the city move pale blind creatures. Above it the fanfare of light. From a distance it is a large whiteness into which the blue bleeds and spreads, a message on blotting paper. From a distance the houses are a tiny colourful scribble on a huge glass plate.

STONE STEPS LEAD into the canal water, the footpath is spangled with petals, wet leaves. Water, earth and plants join to form a walkway. Torcello mosaic floors, sunken and subsided, modeled on shadow play and light pool dapples, the surface of stagnant ponds in autumn, green scum dotted with yellow leaves, twigs, insect larvae, rotting flower heads, water lilies; field mice on the banks dart in and out between tufts of tough grasses. As we walk, the soles of our feet read the floor, it tells of fluctuations of the telluric surface tension. Touch and go. Sorrow for the mortal materiality of the world. We fix our gaze on the divine but Satan appears to shovel sinners into his five greedy jaws, the antichrist reclines in his lap and the golden walls tilt into irrefutable silence.

SOME YEARS ARE GRIEF-STRICKEN as bereft parents, the years when the great silver poplars along the highways lean over in the light as their roots lift slowly from the dust. When the distances between shadows grow and grow. Years when all the rooms are cleared out and the empty walls shimmer green as mould. Beneath the cold glamour of a vodka advertisement, polar bears on ice floes, beneath a billboard displaying famished children the breezes, heavy with golden dreams, caress dry stunted weeds, the brown feet of the women walking there. If we are filled to the brim with dark light like wine chalices, if we are full of gratitude, we are also full of a sorrow as immense as a glass desert.

IN THE LAST JUDGMENT (San Gimignano) the damned are pushed by hell's henchmen into the eternal fires. Some are sentenced from birth to a life in hell. There is such confusion in the streets among rush hours and light rails, and those in charge, policemen and stewards, the stalwarts who conduct the disorderly orchestra, hide their faces behind huge black handlebar moustaches. Among tinsel and serious decor, among the stabled creatures and renaissance straw the children abandon their childish games and hand in their resignations.

THE LANGUAGE OF SPRUCE, trees are exclamation marks on the precipice above the Saracen sea, a blinding turquoise, Lebanon cedars, Scotch pines, yews, but also poplars, stone oaks, balancing the midday, light as a corona of feathers. On the beach a girl in a giraffe bikini slipped into something wild, two boys whistled and a hapless black Ulysses went astray among the sirens. Buses full of pickpockets departed daily from the cathedral where the old men sat in the shade. The young woman beside me on the bus who was plugged into another universe wore a sheer blouse over her shorts and a thin red necklace from Bruges. She was so beautiful that even her freckles were celestial, a fine spray of golden constellations. I had seen her before in the Rijksmuseum skating on the ice hand in hand with her cavalier. The bus driver worshipped her through his rear mirror as we climbed a slope towards a dark pine forest. Behind us in the distance lay the coast of Africa.

HALLUCINATORY WHITE CITY climbing the slopes, twilight of merchants and bankers. Silver rails run along the quays from the synagogue to the Roman theatre, from the tall sinister grain stores along the harbour to the camp nearby, San Sabba. If one only remembered the aroma of ground coffee in the Kaffeehaus San Marco. The busy world ended here. Nothing was ready-made, the objects were beautiful, dignified, crystal chandeliers, polished dishes, and conversations were measured among the rustle of footsteps.

SMALL HUMAN BIOTOPES grow up daily in this city between building site hoardings, stalls offer grilled sausages, beer. Thick-set women, bleached blondes talking incessantly, serve underworld delights, hot mustard, aromatic wines, blandishments. The citizens are wild for light, anything that flickers, ignites, catches flame, for ribbons of light, the peace-keeping army of stars streaming across roof tops, the great fireworks in summer that consume the night.

THOUGHT IS EQUAL to a face pressed against the window glass or a figure standing on the vagrant lawn outside, freezing cold and naked. Do we always want to see damnation followed by redemption? Is it true we can't dream ourselves into a place in heaven? Let us not despair of grace, let us spend tranquil moments, watching cars cross a bridge from left to right and right to left, the water below dark and cross-hatched with small glints, moments akin to peace almost. The odd swan passes turning his quizzical head from side to side. The beautiful ancient complaisance of light and movement, fluidity.

THE SUMMER TICKS OFF the days one by one on its hot blue clipboard. Flowering thorn bushes ignite in barrack yards. The Bosporus laps the feet of the children on the playgrounds, of head-scarfed immigrants, emigrants and waterfowl alike, bee-stings mark blank pages with the blood of innocents and tar melts below glass domes. The elegies of glazed tiles, the outrage of veterans taking mock-pictures of themselves with their arms around naked bodies of strangers, a soldier pretending to eat the spilled brains of a dead Iraqi with a brown plastic spoon.

AT DAWN ON CAPE COD the world is for a moment put to order again, the untiring sun goes about its daily work, free chairs yawn outside the tennis courts, a flat bluish-green sheet stretches all the way to the horizon where a shoal of mackerel climbs the sky. Sand sweepers arrive, the beach-combing machines with their wasp-like hum, turning up the archaeology of summer, tins, towels, half-submerged dinghies. Where have the oars gone? The window blinds of the tabernacle with its shuttered prayer-room creak and flap like early penitents in the breeze. The occasional white point of a sail way out crosses the blue eye of a demigod in denims enthroned on his four-wheel. An osprey tests its wingspan, takes the updraft with lop-sided chutzpah, up and away. As much as you try you can't atone for the thin piercing whine coming from somewhere, the tinnitus in the inner ear of the world, the incessant keening.

I THOUGHT OF the past pressing against the weir with the ton-weight of a rising flood, where I used to swim in the rushing current. Behind me in the power station black turbines churned up the icy green river. In a photograph a bridge floats almost, proud as an ocean ferry with cargoes of passers-by, semi-profiles raised, watching. I thought of wreck buoys with their small cabbalistic lights that flit to and fro past grave excavations along the banks. Some lives assert themselves, gay, agile, lift their fat triangular fins gliding downstream with painted eye, a dolphin's smile that promises nothing. Others have so little appetite for the self, they fade, their minds move with the river, with the silence of fish. Less noticed than air they waft through instruments causing hardly a vibration. The sea is narrower than their faith.

THE CHESTNUT TREES release their light burdens onto the pavement, trembling, they inscribe their shadows on blank firewalls of apartment blocks. From city trains flying past I see them, stand-offish as bears, rooted to the spot in courtyards inside silvery grey galaxies of dust and sparrow twitter, subject to the stoic progress of the bark beetle, the peacock's eye larva. A constant pounding beneath the ground, a heartbeat, a driving force, an internal circulation spirals upwards from roots into delicate leaf veins. Their top branches finger the sky, attach small green flags to it. Life is overpowered by regularity, praise to the variegated, the five-point star, refuge of birds, the wary shuttle-eye in the hedgerows where unruliness thrives. Kafka waiting for the gift of words the night brings. The obsolete beloved nouns—gift, redemption, home, star, love—lie piled up beneath snowdrifts of dead vocabulary.

⁂

ARCHITECTURE OF LIGHT and air. One morning in the town of Ochrid with its three hundred and sixty-five rose-walled churches and mosques, its spires and minarets glittering in the lucid air coming off Lake Ochrid, my brother and I, barely awake and wandering the narrow Osmanian streets on the quest for coffee, felt that there still are undivided places where reason and humanity dwell, nothing was ready-made here, nothing emerged from ugly apparatuses by some warped magic as Canetti describes. We seek out holy scenes everywhere, places of refuge and longing where the soul can rest, the well on Omey below ground in its bed of rounded stones, the stones rounded and polished by the hands of the tide, placed around the trickling source by a tide of hands. In a documentary I saw below the holy city a frieze of figures, early Christian angels, their exalted Giotto profiles and sketchy wings appear on the tunneled excavations and fade almost as quickly again. The young archaeologists lifted their torch lights to catch them before colours and outlines vanished—was it due to sudden contact with light and air?—before the rough walls returned their gaze, grey and ominous. Then all stepped out of the earth into the night streets, into the drum roll of dozens of motorbikes revving up.

⁂

WHAT I LOOK FOR in a painting is not necessarily the finished scene, the portrait or landscape, or a composition but what has been rejected, drawn on the back of the canvas, what has been painted over, first hesitant sketches, charcoal lines ending mid-air, a seated figure where now a window opens into the garden, a drama stopped mid-act, half a profile, a mirror in which the painter portrayed himself where a half open door had been, the head of a woman from whose hands a letter falls. I don't know if she will tear it up or reread it in her own good time.

⁂

FROM MIDDAY LIFE, from quays teeming with coffee tables, citrus trees, suitcases, from lanes full of shouts and laughter we walk into calm submarine grey. The walls, blue-veined, marbled as cold limbs, rise up high to two small apertures below the ceiling that admit one blinding ray each. We stand still, nothing is ours here, none of the stories; we lean against each other, figurines in a tall box lined with Antwerpian baptismal lace which has been tilted and set on its side. The door swings shut, cutting out the day's glare and music. The ceiling vault is hung with clusters of sun and dust, brocaded pendants, golden coils, five-hundred-year-old nests of pulsing shadows. No words have been spoken yet, will perhaps never be spoken. Nothing has to be retracted, nothing changed. Eventually the angel will put his long elegant foot forward shifting the pleats of his skirt in a gesture of breathtaking force, she will recoil, step back lifting her hands to eye-level with her delicate features. How can we leave them behind?—his terrible message, her reluctant obedience, the saint with dreadlocks who cradles a crow, his habit of scratchy wool tied with a scrolled knot, the martyred girl in her school dress? Beyond the door travellers swarm up the sweeping white stairs, houses list to one side, subsiding balustrades lean into the water from which birds drink above their capsized shivering reflections.

A ZEN GARDEN by the sea, boulders, cuckoo flowers, lichen and sea pink clusters, a patch of bearded iris, all arranged according to the design of the master of woodcuts and for my inexpressible delight beside a small marshy pond with a deep-green below-surface shimmer in which lighter green spears stand in relaxed formation. A two-seater plane unravels a silvery skein across the blue above and each lark is lifted upwards by its own airy design, its shipshape calling, its accurate musical métier that thrills us. Fields within perimeters of barbed white hawthorn froth stretch out beneath my feet and the stones in my pocket sing of patience and courage, of finding the lowest level in the rock pool.

ON ITS MARGINS between 19th century power stations, incinerators and run-down boulevards named after the empress, the city slowly dies. The thisness of tall windowless walls, arsenals, prisons, graveyards filled with their inanimate selves. In the reptile shop Meister Tod reclines curled around his own dead centre, muscular, his coiled interlacings shine with intricate markings. He has a ferocious appetite: inside his hypnotic eye a cowering miniature rabbit shivers before the sacrifice. I am invited to purchase him or something mysterious next-door, what the hairdressers promise as a

'Millenial Style'. Beside a shuttered nameless night club the paltry red heart of the Eros centre flashes on and off drawing me to it. I feel its despairing heat, it longs to outlive my death.

            *

THE GREAT CITIES, conquered, destroyed, burnt down, rebuilt, plundered, sectioned, auctioned, sold, modernized. In side streets in dark shops we buy nostalgia. All afternoon in the summer heat I remembered the attic: slate tiles, burning hot to the touch, wreckage, bundled letters, grand-mother's china, silver, tarnished and bent, books mouldering, camphor in coat pockets, archives of lead submerged in the dust that caused me to cough and sneeze and my skin to break out in an angry red rash, a pre-first-world-war student's cap with gold-braided trim—my grandfather's?— photo albums, snapshots of black forests, seaside outings, an officer—my uncle—young and handsome on horseback, the photograph of Rabbi Kitteler on the banks of the Rhine, a small square picture with scalloped white edges, beneath it his name written in grandmother's hand with white ink on thick grey paper— her good friend, was he on one of the trains setting out from the deportation ramp, track 17 in Grunewald station? A stream of motes danced below the open skylight and the dirty lamps of wasps' nests hung in the rafters, fragile, eerie structures, almost weightless, shredded and sprinkled with fine grey powder; the cells and sections built with the ingenuity of city architects giving these complex globes their shape and cohesion were vacant, emptied of their much maligned community.

            *

IN CHICAGO GARDENS a bird with cinnabar wings sang into my ear and I wrote it all down: precise trills and grace notes mingled with the plainsong of the city, the squirrels that swung among the branches of the sorrow tree, the cat near the crown keeping bird, squirrel and me well within view with its crescent eyes. Meanwhile the divine painter was busy applying gold leaf to the margins of the sky and blue enamel to the tips of delphiniums. Beside the runway in the airport an orange windbag floated above its pole filled to bursting with inspiration one minute and hung slack and empty as the bellows of a silent organ the next. This was the quiet centre of July—pauses fell between steep reflecting buildings in the long streets near Lake Michigan, only a low-pitched chorus could still be heard *unisono* through a small window high above the transept in a ruined abbey, the sound threading through the ear of a needle. If I crossed a nettle and thistle field and climbed a tall ladder to the window I would see the rock-strewn islands of the Connemara coast, the crested towers of ist waves. And perched on top the window's pointed arch, sun-warmed and grey, three monks chanting, egg-bald, beating time with their sandalled feet.

AN ICE BUCKET turned over slowly on a table in the park café, glacial water dripped into newsprint, the words *death camps, mass graves* barely glimpsed. The destructive force of words against unshaken belief. Sophie Scholl dreams the night before her execution that she gently lays down the child she has been carrying in her arms across a snowfield before she plunges into the glacial crevasse. If music and courtesy were understood, says Confucius, there would be no more war. The healing force of music, even only of scales being practised, running up and down, minor, major, impromptus, modulations, late Beethoven *Opus 32,* in two movements, the transition from C-minor to C-major, the musical scale of light, taking a last look around, taking leave, transcending the pain of departure.

A BEAUTIFUL USEFUL WORD in German *Zeitraum* combines time and space in one. Does this not encapsulate the way memory works? Childhood railway journeys to cities of memory, with their long streets, marketplaces, fences, buildings and rooms, our arrival beneath steamed-up glass vaults: I hold my aunt's leather-gloved fingers, she is wearing her maroon hat with a veil and a jay feather, her stern eye detects flecks of coal dust on my cheek, wipes it with a lace handkerchief she has daintily spat on. The sour smell of her saliva, my cheek feels hot, my hand surreptitiously touches it, I fear a visible mark. The aroma of hot steel, anthracite and boiled frankfurters. Station are embodiments of Zeitraum—here time and space converge and disperse, the world, the years come and go. Coffee-drinkers in the dark restaurant sit silent with their eyes on the shiny brass wall clock, Monsieur Chronos among them, waiting for the Orient Express.

THE PAST IS THERE, omnipresent, in flux, outside on the tree-lined boulevard, the flowering lindens' narcotic scent and airborne fluff adrift above the neck of the cab horse as it trots along the street, its head nodding in prayer. Families on the greens, a jovial baritone sings *when your grandda courted your grandma*, a brass band marches past behind serious handlebar moustaches, cymbals, trumpets and drumbeat making a comical clamour on the way to the pavilion. By the pond the understated Japanese glamour of drakes. Could this be a false memory—the sweetshop in the lane where we buy pralines imprinted with the face of young Amadeus? I can see the sparrows picking through dung and dust, smell the stench of horse sweat rising, sudden and sharp after the parade. We walk past citizens who sip liqueurs in the cafés, past the crackle of starched linen, the paper headlines report uprisings in distant provinces but the newsprint only darkens fingers, not the general mood. Zeitraum of images—an imperial hand waves from a window, grandmother and her friends float gaily past in ivory silks, their young lives cradled in the crooks of their arms like overblown roses. The lindens shower them with fruit, small as hard as grapeshot. On the dot of twelve a glockenspiel cuts loose in the clock tower, scatters notes like ammunition on the square.

⁂

FAST FORWARD TO THE PRESENT: the airport of a city struck with amnesia, a late arrival, taxi drivers have taken the night off, light rails stopped running long ago. There was a war here just recently, reason-defying and bloody, where one part of the inhabitants drove out or murdered the other. On our way through dimly lit streets and across cobbled squares we see former imperial grandeur crumbling everywhere, illegible road-signs, boarded-up doors and windows, buildings of state like decrepit gigantic toads hidden behind construction hoardings. Among the mirrors and fake gold, cold looks and stares in the hotel lobby we attempt a greeting in the local vernacular and are ignored. No one wants us here, tourists with the wrong currency in our pockets. (Do we not know this city, we have been here before, wasn't there snow on the ground, shops were shuttered, tracks of military vehicles crisscrossed the square?) At last the surly manager takes us to our basement room where a musty smell—of something undefinable, decay or putrefaction?—keeps us awake all night. Over breakfast in a nearby bar we wonder what we came for, ponder maps of an ancient burial ground perhaps where thousand-year-old bones lie unearthed in the crypt of a basilica. Burnt-out wrecks of armoured trucks are piled up against the barrack walls, mass graves are excavated as we order tea and the stage is being set for the next war. The woman who sits ranting on the curb, the ex-soldier begging from passers-by are the latest or last recruits in the city's ghostly parade of the lost, and I ask myself, my face in my hands, will nothing ever redeem the past?

The Drowned Book

> *... deeper than did ever plummet sound*
> *I'll drown my book*
> —Prospero in Shakespeare's *The Tempest.* Act V Scene 1

Hidden in a cave of leaves
I spent my childhood reading high above
the garden's afternoon ritual

where the lion of summer snored
under the table and coffee was served.
Letters followed one another

black and ant-like across the page forming words,
a trail of sweetness towards a major key
that smelled of sailors and apples from China.

The Goddess of Silence lived in the garden
and her sisters Forgetting and Invention,
stern, calico-clad, laurel-wreathed,

weaving pictograms into durable snares,
Assyrian, hook and braid, stone jug, owl,
water pot, ibis, fox fur.

I was hooked, lost to the world, my mother's call,
my brothers' games, football, hide and seek.
Poems ignited in my heart,

they were a freshly opened jar
of condiments, a planet-cluster
settling on a gate, a snowdrift piling up.

I would read till dawn.
My father would catch me at four
with the light still on.

I'd been to the sources of night and found
the magic book
the sorcerer Prospero had drowned.

Lacrimae rerum

GERMAN JOKES ARE no laughing matter, people always tell me. True, my country's national emblem is the teardrop. Our anthem is composed of sobs and wails. Our chancellor Lugubrius Herzschmerz is a graduate of the Academy of Fine Keening. General Cri de Coeur heads the defence forces. Laughter is against the law, so are cheers, jubilees, merriment, revels, frolics, larks, horseplay, high jinks and any form of foolery. Smilers, grinners, smirkers, snickerers, titterers, cacklers and gigglers are punished. The prisons are full of jokers, funny men and women, ironists, satirists, clowns and buffoons. Lie-down tragedians perform on hospital trolleys which are wheeled onto the stage as they draw their last breath. The audience is routinely handed boxes of tissues with the tickets. Funerals are our favourite entertainments, they last for days and are so crowded that riot police erect punch-line barriers. Music is plucked on our heartstrings. We sleep wet-eyed in wet blankets, we drink dampened spirits. Our songs are swan songs and requiems. Theatre bills features tragedies, or the Lives of the Martyrs only. Popular family outings are to the Vale of Tears, a lightless place with a precipice where tear dropping contests are held. The most copious ducts and best boo-hoos, moans, whimpers, whines or bawls get the prize. Poets only compose elegies, composers funeral marches. Acrobats in sackcloth and ashes take the heart out of each other. In combat hostile armies tear each other's hair, wring each other's hands and beat each other's breasts until one side dissolves in floods of tears. From the crocodiles in the zoo to the worms in the can every creature weeps. "We suffer sadness gladly," I reply, sniffling into my handkerchief.

Snow Story

If I had one wish it would be
to have been born two or three
hundred years earlier in Japan.

I'd adopt a new name:
Banana Tree or Blue Ink Pot,
or even Cup of Tea

and talk to crickets and swallows
knowing that the Milky Way
was reflected in their eyes, too.

I might take to the road,
the one to the Deep North
or live in seclusion complaining of too many visitors.

I would study how a tree
stands for itself and nothing else
and try to learn from it.

I'd teach important things
like ideograms, meaning *polite frog*
or *snail climbing Mount Fuji*

and on my wanderings fix my broken sandal thongs
or tears in my knapsack,
listening to the small songs of the insects.

At the end of my life I might find myself alone
living in a grain store with snow
falling through holes in the roof.

Memoir

THE STORY OF MY LIFE will never be written and my readers will never read it. It is by the obscure but famous author Anon and has been out of print for years. Even if you go into the dustiest libraries or archives in obscure little mining towns in Pennsylvania or in Minsk, down into the dankest cellars where the heating pipes provide the ideal habitat for spiders and cockroaches you won't find a shred of it. It is a memoir set in the distant future in the golden buckwheat fields of Poland. Its main characters are a dancing bear, three monkeys, a woman driving a tour bus, an old accordion player and a few little star-handed bar girls. The climate of my memoir is unpredictable. The language is unfamiliar, some think it is a Swedish swindle, others a Latvian lie, but you know how sensitive the critics are. The valleys of the novel are dotted with watermills, floodgates, rainbow traps, icicle presses and factories with assembly lines where snowflakes are fashioned, trillions of them, each according to its individual design. Here the weather is produced that drifts to us and sweeps and billows in the weeping willows. Solitary people on mountain tops free storms or dark clouds from small silver cages or they stuff the tiniest sun rays that still exist into fishing nets and throw them to the roaches. The plot is so confusing that it rains incessantly and tornado follows on hurricane. The main protagonist is a very old Persian poet who, during the nightly cloudbursts, dances tango with a bar girl on the wooden pier of a lake, toasting the moon in iambic Farsi. He has invented a musical scale in which all sorrowful music sounds happy and all slow songs fast and vice versa. In the evenings when east-and west-flying planes drag their thin grey vapour trails across the sky he shelters behind a shellac screen made from thousands of beetle wings. The red drops dripping onto the tarmac from the screen are gathered at sunset and made into roses for the wedding feast which is always tomorrow.

Kōan

We are waiting in the café beside the station high above the old
    town,
there will be no trains, everyone is out

on strike. Our glasses sparkle in the midday sun. With a gentle
    growl
the cases of other passengers roll past

towards the station or the old town. We know nothing.
Somewhere in an open-plan office

full of frightened or irritated faces phone calls are made, news
    passed on.
It is so easy to fall out of the present.

The abbey in Souillac is squat and heavy, slow-moving,
curved and armoured as a tortoise

with whom it shares its wisdom and age. The old women
circle around it like jackdaws,

their shopping bags full of messages and sorrow. We watched them
from our hotel window which faces

the back of the abbey. We have seen Isaiah's winged cloak, the
    marble
lace hem, the ecstatic folds of the gathered fabric,

his hair plaited into narrow plaits and his wild long beard.
How hard it must be to be blind

and yet to see the future, clear and illuminated by the morning
    light
into which small song birds

hang their intricate embroideries. The iconoclasts have broken
    the light
of his eyes with their hammers

and chisels but though they are practiced defacers they could
    not destroy
the moment of vision and revelation.

Despite the explosives the great Buddhas are still there guarding
    their valley,
no note written by Bach or Monteverdi can be made

unheard. All around Isaiah—above and beside him—rages
the judgement. Evil devours itself in many-headed

demonic intertwined forms, the devils wear delicate beaded
skirts to cover their shame, Isaac

leans his young head into the crook of his father's arm whose
    other arm
is already lowering the knife.

Last night, at midnight after the street lamps were extinguished,
the apse windows turned towards us

fluted and black. The square was empty, only the
continuous *poc poc poc*

of a tennis ball could be heard: a single player in an empty court
in darkness, fog and silence.

The Piano Player's Resumé

There's not much longevity in being a star
so I wore different musical hats.
My family spoke many tuneful languages
but I took a sabbatical early

and stayed at home for eighteen years.
It is good to be there
for your children. They taught me
how the soul can sing, aflame and innocent

to itself alone. After years dedicated to sound
the gist of my wisdom is
to be as silent as I can
especially in autumn when dirges

are piped through the capillaries
of a million shedding trees
when the light turns shrill around the edge
and a sharper key is played.

We only talk of births and deaths now
when we meet old friends. Surgery,
radiation, a new set of baby teeth.
The cathedral doors are open

and steps lead down into the stone
vaults where organ pipes root. Someone treads
the bellows, hard and fast, all my life
I have never been able to see the face.

But when I do, how I will be aflame—
how I will sing.

NOTES

Page 9: '&' is the symbol for the ligature of the two letters, *e* and *t,* of the word *et,* Latin for *and.* Its present form is much the same as the one used in Carolingian minuscule writing of the 9th century. I am indebted to Mark Stansbury, paleographer and lecturer at NUI Galway for drawing my attention to the history of this symbol.

Page 30: 'Achill Killeen': Killeen, an unconsecrated graveyard for unbaptised children. It was folk custom in Ireland to bury babies near a prehistoric grave, a dolmen or passage grave, because 'if the catholic god won't have them, maybe the old gods will'.

Page 34: 'Stendhal Syndrome': a psycho-somatic condition—rapid heart beat, dizziness, racing pulse—experienced on encountering a work of art, or beauty in the natural world. Its name is derived from Stendhal's description of his own extreme physical reactions following his visit to Santa Croce in Florence.

Page 44: 'Jardin Botanico': Ibn al-Baytar, born 1179, died 1248. Famous Andalusian botanist, herbalist and physician, author of such works as *The Ultimate in Materia Medica,* and *The Complete Guide to Basic Medicaments and Nutrition.*

Page 53: 'Homage'. According to the poet, after an illness she experienced daydreams vivid as the ones described and felt it as a loss when they ceased in the course of recovery.

Page 55: 'The poet at ninety writes a letter': Stella Rotenberg, Jewish-Austrian poet, fled to England in 1939 and has lived there since. Her parents were murdered by the Nazis. The last five lines of the poem quote from some of her poems.

Page 75: 'Orplid': an imaginary distant and yearned-for country in German Romanic poet Eduard Mörike's poem 'Gesang Weylas'. Jews who returned to Germany after the Shoah usually found it emotionally difficult to settle back into their former homes and left again, to Israel or the US. Most had grown up steeped in German culture, German romantic poetry, Goethe, Heine or Mörike for example. During the Nazi years the passports of Jews were marked with a J.

List of Illustrations
by Miriam de Burca

Cover image: Native Alien Forest
The Soul of the Piano: Oxford Ragwort
The Grass Garden: Reed Canary Grass
Travelling with Ruby: Willow Herb
The Heart of Things: Spear Thistle
Journal from the Mirrored Cities: Pepperwort

Dedalus Press
Poetry from Ireland and the world

Established in 1985, the Dedalus Press is one of Ireland's best-known literary imprints, dedicated to new Irish poetry and to poetry from around the world in English translation.

For further information on Dedalus Press titles, as well as audio samples and podcasts in our Audio Room, please visit **www.dedaluspress.com**.

"One of the most outward-looking poetry presses in Ireland and the UK"
—UNESCO.org

Lightning Source UK Ltd.
Milton Keynes UK
04 April 2011

170367UK00001B/77/P